# The Great Discovery

*by*

Norman Maclean

# The Great Discovery
## by Norman Maclean

Copyright © 2024

All Rights reserved.



ISBN: 978-93-61428-44-9

**Published by**

# DOUBLE 9 BOOKS

2/13-B, Ansari Road
Daryaganj, New Delhi – 110002
info@double9books.com
www.double9books.com
Tel. 011-40042856

This book is under public domain

# ABOUT THE AUTHOR

Norman Maclean, a renowned novelist and scholar, is most famous for his timeless masterwork, "The Great Discovery." Maclean, who was born with a deep love of nature and a strong eye for detail, frequently explores themes of human connection, personal growth, and the secrets of the natural world in his creative works. In "The Great Discovery," Maclean leads readers on a transforming voyage of self-discovery and enlightenment. Through emotional prose and lyrical storytelling, he explores the fundamental intricacies of the human experience. Set against the backdrop of the breathtaking wilderness, "The Great Discovery" recounts the protagonist's search for meaning and purpose in the majesty and quiet of nature. As the story progresses, readers are transported into a world of introspection and revelation, where profound insights emerge and life-changing discoveries are made. Maclean's command of words and ability to convey the sights, sounds, and experiences of the natural world are unrivaled. He transports readers to a world of wonder and amazement with his descriptive descriptions and emotive images, infusing each moment with significance and purpose. "The Great Discovery" exemplifies Maclean's literary genius and lasting significance as a writer.

# CONTENTS

# Preface

Six articles which the writer contributed to *The Scotsman* constitute this book. Four of these, which appeared under the title "In Our Parish," were, in response to requests, re-printed by *The Scotsman* as leaflets, and in that form had a circulation that reached an aggregate of 100,000. One of the articles (now Chapter II.), which was published on February 14, 1914, has been revised and somewhat enlarged. The rest are reprinted substantially as they were originally written.

In these last months there has come to the nation a spiritual and ethical revival. Life will never again be what it was in the last long summer days ere the guns began to speak. It will be a better world than it has yet been. The nation is being saved as by fire, and in the fire much dross will be consumed. The conscience of the State has been stirred, and it cannot in the future acquiesce in the continuance of the social evils which are gnawing at the nation's heart. The fate of the Empire in the long years to come will depend more on the fight for social renewal in the midst of the streets than on red battlefields. To the men who have stood between the race and destruction the State owes a debt which it can only repay by such measures of social regeneration as will make possible for every man and woman to realise the thrill and the joy of life. These pages only represent an effort to portray the first stirring of that newly awakened consciousness of God and of duty which was felt in every parish throughout the Empire, and which is destined to transform the world.

# I
# The Great Discovery

While the thing is still fresh in my mind I will try to put it down on paper—the incredible thing that has happened in our parish. When we had least thought about life's great things, we have come face to face with the greatest.

We had been for long years living on the surface of things. The sun basked on the slopes of the hills, purple at eve; we came back from the offices in town, plunged through the tunnel, and hastened to our gardens. We lifted up our eyes to the hills, and our security seemed as immovable as their crests soaring above the little dells that were haunts of ancient peace around their foundations.

Long years of ease dimmed our vision. The church bell rang in vain for many of us. Those who had six whole days in the week to devote to their own pleasure began to devote the seventh also to that same end. The day of peace was becoming a day of unrest.

Thus it was with us when, with the suddenness of a lightning flash, the incredible overtook us.

If only one could put it into words! But words can never express this sudden meeting of man and God when that meeting was least expected.

It was heralded by the booming of guns across the sea. The great city lay slumbering between us and the shore, but over the turrets and spires it came—boom, boom—under the stars. It was war. That far-away echo might not itself be the grim struggle of death, but it was its harbinger. Over all the seas death would soon be riding on the billows. Faces became stern. Good-byes were spoken.

Ah! that word "Good-bye," which we hear every day, and which, like those old coins which have passed from hand to hand so long until at last the image and superscription are gone, had lost all trace of its original meaning, retaining nothing but a faint aroma of courtesy, which sometimes vanished in the inflection of the voice until the word became only a discourteous dismissal—that word was born for us anew. We heard it on the lips of mothers clinging to the hands of their sons, who were summoned away to join their regiments, and as white lips said "Good-bye" to those whose blood was to water the fair fields of France, we suddenly realised what it meant. The word, meaningless yesterday, to-day expressed the greatest wish that the lips of man can utter—God be with thee. On the mother's lips the word was the commitment of her boy to the charge of the encompassing God. Then, when the harvest was ripening on the slopes and the drum sounded "Come," and the young and the strong went forth with a smile to the great harvesting of death, we learned again the meaning of a phrase. But we were yet to learn the meaning of a word.

It is in the darkness that the stars appear and the immeasurable abysses of the infinite universe, and it was when the dusk sank into the deep night that the word rose high in the firmament of life and burned red into our souls. And that word was God.

It seemed so incredible to us that we should need that old word. We were so powerful and so rich. Our faith was strong, but it was in the reeking tube and in the smoking shard, and in the number of our Dreadnoughts. Then all these things seemed to fail us. A nightmare seemed to fall on us—a nightmare which lifted not night or day. Our soldiers were driven back, back, back. They fought by day and marched by night, and we heard in the night watches the beating of their wearied feet, blood stained.

Was there to be no end to that tramp, tramp of men yielding before death? Was the Empire reared by the heroism of generations to crumble under our feet? The ghastly deeds of shame—were they to come to our doors! We looked at our children, and they could not understand the light in our eyes. These deeds of hell—they might occur even now under the shadow of our hills. It was then that the word began to blaze in the heavens. And the word was—God.

We had built a new church in our parish, that those who built pleasant houses on the slopes, fleeing from the restless city that lay below, might have room to worship. But the desire to worship seemed to be dying of attrition. And the old church where the quarriers and farm servants assembled and worshipped in an atmosphere that on a warm day became so thick that one could cut it with a knife—that old church would have been quite big enough to hold all who came, for the instinct to pray seemed to be dying. And many, because the new church was now too big, regretted the old.

Then, suddenly, the new church was filled to the door. Men and women discovered the road leading down to the hollow where the church stands amid the graves of the generations. With wistful faces they turned towards it. While the bell rang they stood in groups among the graves. And if you listened there was but one word—war, war, war. Over and over again just that one word. Until the bell was silent, and they turned into the now crowded church.

As I sat there and cast a glance around me, I felt a sudden amazement. Those who never before had come down the steep brae when the bell was ringing were sitting here and there just as if they had been there every Sunday when the beadle, with head erect, ushers the minister to the pulpit and snips him in. (Though the church is new, the minister is yet snipped in by the beadle—a lonely prisoner there on his perch, and it is an uncanny sound to hear the click of that snip shutting in the solitary man.)

In the pew in front of me sat a burly man with a head like a dome. He never came to church. When I met him he would stand for an hour in the lane among the hawthorns explaining his views. Prayer was mere superstition. Cosmic laws unchanging and unchangeable held the universe in their grasp. To ask that one of these laws should be altered for a moment that a boon might be conferred on us was to ask that the universe might be shattered. Prayer was immoral, the asking for what could not be granted, and what we knew could not be granted. If he went to church it would be hypocrisy on his part.

And thus it came that when the farm servants came up the Gallows road on their way to church on a summer morning, they often heard the whirr of my friend's mowing machine as he mowed his lawn. It was the way he took of letting the parish know that culture could have no dealings with effete superstitions.

And yet there he sat in front of me with a hymn-book which he picked up from the shelf at the door, where such books are piled for the use of camp-followers. The tune of the opening Psalm was Kilmarnock, and my friend sang it in a way which showed that his mother had trained him well. Then I forgot him, but after a while something like a stifled sob in front of me brought him again to my consciousness.

The minister began to pray for the King's forces "on the sea, on the land, and in the air." My mind was playing round the words "in the air," for they were an intrusion into the familiar order—an innovation! Every invention of man seemed doomed to become a weapon in the hand of the devil. But the prayer went on—for the sailors keeping their watches in the darkness of the night that God might watch over them, that through their unfaltering courage our shores might be inviolate; for the soldiers now facing the enemy, grappling with death, that God might succour them, covering their heads in the day of battle. "Break Thou down the fierce power of our enemies," cried the minister suddenly, "that with full hearts we may praise Thee, the God of our fathers."

A great hush fell on the crowded church. The shut eyes saw the red battlefields, with the lines swaying to and fro, while the shrapnel burst and the aeroplanes whirred in the smoke of the cannon. The cries of men suddenly smitten smote on the inner ear. It was then that the great thing happened.

All of a sudden the voice broke, recovered, and broke again, and the minister was swept away from the well-ordered, beautiful words he had prepared. He began to speak of the stricken hearts at home, of fathers and mothers to whom their sons would never return, of women in empty houses with their husbands laid in nameless graves, of little children who would never learn to say "Father" ... It was then that my friend stifled a sob. There was Something after all, Someone greater than cosmic forces, greater than law—with an eye to pity and an arm to save. There was God.

And my friend's son was with the famous regiment that was swaying to and fro, grappling with destiny. He was helpless—and there was only God to appeal to. There comes an hour in life when the heart realises that instinct is mightier far than that logic which is, after all is said, only the last refuge of the feeble-minded. There came like the sudden lifting of a curtain the vision of a whole nation—nay, of races girdling the whole earth—to whom the same high experience has come. Everywhere the sanctuaries filled, the eyes turned upward, for instinct is mightier than reason. The smoke of battle has revealed the face of God.

With us in the parish churches of Scotland the great thing is the sermon. But to-day it is different; the great thing now is prayer. And the minister preached about prayer. He set forth in clear and ordered language, with a felicitous phrase now and then lighting up his sentences, that prayer was not a mere relic of fanatical superstition but a mighty power. He discussed with a wealth of learning whether God had shut Himself in behind a prison-house of cosmic laws that made it impossible for Him to answer prayer. He reasoned the worshippers cold. But there in that hour reason was bound to give way before intuition.

"If I am free," cried the preacher, "to rush to the help of my child when he crieth in terror; and if, when the creatures of His hand cry to God He is bound and cannot help or soothe, then He is poorer than I, so great a thing is freedom." Prayer was not mere spiritual gymnastics. A God immured in cold laws, barred for ever from the play of love or tenderness, would be the one being in the universe most to be pitied. The Creator did not sit deaf and dumb on the Throne of indifference answering nothing, doing nothing. History was the proof that Righteousness was throned at the core of the universe, for at the last right ever prevailed.

Then the measured tones went on to speak of the difficulty of believing in the efficacy of prayer when Christians faced Christians in mortal conflict, and they both cried for victory—both the children of the One Father crying for victory over each other. But the difficulty was of appearance only. For the only prevailing prayer was prayer in the name of Christ. "Whatsoever ye shall ask *in My name* that will I do." To ask in His name was to ask in His spirit—the spirit of humility, self-sacrifice, and love—the spirit of self-surrender to the *will* supreme. The question was which of the prayers for victory was prayer in the name of Christ....

This was clear, convincing, but cold. Only at rare intervals does the minister of our parish give way to passion. Suddenly there came a wave of emotion. He flung his head back, and his eyes glowed. His voice vibrated through the church. "When I think," he exclaimed, "of the things that have been done with the name of God on men's lips; of atrocities such as the unspeakable Turk never perpetrated; of war waged not upon to-day but upon the centuries of faith that reared great cathedrals now in flames; of women and children laid upon the reeking altars of human passion; and all this in the name of culture, the culture of the superman who deems himself superior to the Ten Commandments—then, I say, may God grant that the culture which beareth such fruit may perish from off the face of the earth. Prayer for the triumph of such a cause cannot be in Christ's name...."

But the preacher never got any further.

This was what happened, and I am afraid some will not believe me, for a Scotsman in church is a stoic, motionless and dumb, as he listens to the Word. But all the traditions of the parish were snapped in a second. In the side gallery sat the General, sitting as he always does with his back to the minister. This he does that he may mark who are in church of his servants and tenants, and who absent.

When I read of the nobles in France who went to the scaffold with a jest in the days of the Terror, I always think of the General. He is that sort of man. To-day, little by little, as the sermon went on, he turned round. At last he was facing the pulpit. His gleaming eyes were fixed on the preacher. His son was dead. And when the words rang through the church, may God grant that such culture may perish ... the General sprang to his feet. "Amen" rang his voice through the church.

There was a sudden movement; as one man they all rose to their feet. Hands were lifted up to heaven. "Amen," "Amen," they cried— and then there rose a cheer—muffled, but still a cheer. In the pulpit the words died on the preacher's lips. He seemed as one suddenly stricken. He gazed bewildered over the sea of faces. They sank back into the pews as though suddenly ashamed.

The last man to sit was my friend, who stood to the last with uplifted hand. I think it was he who cried "Hear, hear"—the only sign he gave of his long absence from church. The sermon was never finished. The preacher in a low voice said, "Let us pray." And he humbled himself as one who enters the valley of humiliation. And then he gave out this psalm:—

> Now Israel
> May say, and that truly,
> If that the Lord
> Had not our cause maintained;
> *   *   *   *   *
>
>
> Then certainly
> They had devoured us all.
> *   *   *   *   *
>
>
> But blessed be God,
> Who doth us safely keep,
> And hath not giv'n
> Us for a living prey
> Unto their teeth,
> And bloody cruelty.
> *   *   *   *   *

This psalm as we sang it that day was a pæan of triumph. The clouds suddenly broke. We heard our fathers singing it in their dark days. The melody wedded to the words soared in exultant triumph, wailed like the cry of the shingle swept by the surf; the sighing of the wind over the heather was in it, and the hissing of the storm through the spray. It was fierce as devouring death; it was gentle as a mother crooning over her child. It put iron into the blood of our fathers as they sang it.

It was nerved by such a hymn that the sailors of Queen Elizabeth swept the main, that the Puritans wrestled with principalities and powers, that a handful of moors-men levelled despotism and tyranny to the ground. It swept through our blood like flame as we in our day of stress now sang it. We, too, would pull down strongholds and turn to flight the armies of the alien. In all ages the cause of freedom triumphed, and that cause was ours. We had entered on conflict with clean hands and, God helping us, we would wage it with clean hands. The clouds suddenly broke and the light of victory irradiated our faces. There came overwhelmingly the realisation that there was a power behind us mightier far than sword or shell—even the Lord God Omnipotent. And that was how we made the greatest of all discoveries—we found God.

Yesterday morning I went early to the station, and there in the booking office I found my friend talking to the ticket-collector. The ticket-collector is a philosopher, and he comes to church, because he loves the old psalm tunes. But when one of our parishioners who goes now and then to Keswick comes to the booking office, the ticket-collector calls him in and reasons with him gently.

"Mahn, there's naething in it," he says; "I can tell you for a fact there's naething in it—all a whack of fables." "Some day you'll find out to your cost that there's something in it," flashes the man from Keswick. "If ye wad only reid philosophee," says the ticket-collector, "ye would ken better." But to-day my friend and the ticket-collector had their heads close together, and I only heard the conclusion of their argument. "Mahn," said the ticket-collector, "I am beginning to think there may be something in it."

And in the evening near the top of the brae I saw the General standing erect with his little cane in his hand. He was talking to the shoemaker, the greatest Radical in the parish—one of a party with which the General has no dealings. But they talked like brothers. For the shoemaker has a son fighting at the front, and his heart is sore troubled within him. And the General's son is dead. And as I came up the brae I saw the General putting his hand on the shoemaker's shoulder and turn away, walking slowly up the brae. The old shoemaker saluted and came down the brae. There was a tender look in the old man's eye as he greeted me.

In our parish we have truly made the greatest of all discoveries. We have found God, and, finding Him, we have found each other. The man who in his madness kindled the lurid flames of war little dreamed of this fire which he kindled.

# II
# The Revival of Patriotism

There has come to us in these days a revival of the spirit of patriotism. That revival has come when it was sorely needed. In days of unclouded prosperity other gods called forth our devotion and enthusiasm, but the God of our Fathers who made us a great nation and sent us to sow the seeds of righteousness beside all waters, bestowing upon us empire and might, was well-nigh forgotten.

For the new man "words like Empire, Patriotism, Duty, Honour, Glory and God" had little or no meaning. Causes for which the fathers died could not evoke an added heart-beat from their sons. They cared so little for the mighty empire which they inherited that they contemplated the bloodshed of civil war—so hot was their zeal for party and so cold their love for the state.

It was necessary that discipline should come. And that discipline came, shaking the very foundations of our national life. Its first fruit is that the smouldering fires of patriotism have broken forth once more into bright flame; and that everywhere the hearts of the people have been stirred by the call to arise and endure hardness that the goodly heritage of empire perish not. And preachers in a thousand pulpits have sounded the trumpet-note of duty and of patriotism.

It has been said that preachers should aim at making the churches sanctuaries of peace, within whose walls the echoes of the guns and the cries of the perishing should not penetrate. Some have even said that Christianity, so far from fostering the spirit of patriotism, is in reality hostile to it. "Patriotism itself as a duty," says Lecky, "has never found any place in Christian ethics, and strong theological feeling has usually been directly hostile to its growth."

No doubt there is something to be said for that view. The attitude of the early Christians towards the Roman Empire was not that of patriotism. The clear shining of the heavenly Jerusalem so dazzled their eyes that this world, and the temporal empire occupying its stage, seemed but as a shadow. Their devotion to the Unseen King left little room for loyalty to the earthly ruler.

In the glorious consciousness of his citizenship in heaven, it was a small thing in the estimation of St. Paul that he was also a Roman citizen—but he did not forget it. But when the earthly ruler persecuted, and burnt, and threw the Christians to the lions, or slaughtered them to make a Roman holiday, then the poor victims cannot be blamed for not being patriots.

And the Church in the mediæval period, organised in the mighty hierarchy of Rome, did not tend to foster a national spirit of patriotism. In those days when the Emperor Theodosius made penance in the Cathedral of Milan and Ambrose declared that "the Church is not in the empire, but the Emperor in the Church"; or in those later days when Hildebrand promulgated the doctrine that the temporal power was subject to the spiritual power, and kings and emperors were only vassals of the Church, and Henry V. was left three days standing barefooted in the snow waiting humbly to see the Pope at Canossa—in those days certainly Christianity sought to foster not the sense of national loyalty, but that of devotion towards that holy Catholic and universal Church whose visible head was the Pope. Christianity placed the Pope on the throne of the Cæsars, and sought to evoke towards him a patriotism which transcended nationality. But the Reformation gave its death blow to Hildebrandism, and the Pope no longer usurped the temporal Thrones of Europe. And there came the throb of the awakening spirit of nationality. The spirit of patriotism stirred once more the slumbering races.

The question whether patriotism is a fruit of Christianity must be answered not by reference to what men did in the name of their religion—for men are fallible—but by the precept and example of the Founder of Christianity. He was a Jew, and of all races the Jew was the most patriotic. An exile by the rivers of Babylon, the Israelite refused to forget Zion. "If I forget thee, O Jerusalem, let my right hand forget its cunning"—that was the cry wherewith his unconquerable soul faced an overwhelming destiny. And in this respect Jesus Christ was true to His race. He was a patriot. He worshipped in the synagogues, and went on pilgrimages to Jerusalem, because He loved the national institutions of His country. One note of true patriotism is anguish. It is when love is great that the folly and sin of the person beloved pierce the heart.

The patriotism of the Founder of Christianity expressed itself in a cry of agony which has reverberated through the centuries—"O Jerusalem, Jerusalem, thou that killest the prophets, and stonest them that are sent unto thee, how often would I have gathered thy children together, even as a hen gathereth her chickens under her wings, and ye would not! Behold, your house is left unto you desolate." That cry is the measure of His patriotism.

Judged, then, by the example of its Founder, Christianity must produce the spirit of love and loyalty towards one's own country. There was a patriotism before Christianity, but it was that of arrogance, aggression, and self-glorification. It was a patriotism which meted out only contempt to other races. To the Jew the Greek was only a Gentile dog; to the Greek the Jew was only a contemptible Barbarian.

But the patriotism which is animated by the Christian spirit is far other. It is not the vaunting of pride nor the shouting of vulgar ditties. It seeks the glory of its own country, but the glory it seeks is the glory of the greater service rendered to humanity. Conscious of its own defects, it does not condemn others. With eyes cleansed from prejudice, it beholds the good in other races. It seeks the first place for its own nation because it acts the noblest, loves the best. All the elements which make up the strong power of patriotism—love of family, love of neighbours, love of race, love of country—Christianity has purified them all. True patriotism is, then, a fruit of the Christian religion, a virtue which falls to be inculcated by the Church. If Christianity be the projection of the Christ-life into the midst of every generation, then the life that reflects the beauty of Christ must be a life animated by the deepest love of one's country.

It was Dean Stanley who rendered God thanks in Paisley Abbey for that Scotsmen were "citizens of an Empire so great, members of a Church so free." In the building up of the Empire Scotsmen have borne a great share of toil and peril. In other days the fires of patriotism burned brightly. The cry of our fathers was "my country right or wrong." But we feel not quite so sure of our country being always in the right. The passion of Christianity is an ethical passion. Christian patriotism demands national righteousness. To keep patriotism as an ardent fire we must be convinced that our country stands for righteousness. And in this day of our ordeal we have this certainty to uphold us, that we are fighting for the right.

It was not in defiance of Christianity, but in its defence, that we drew the sword. For this war sprang from an unbridled lust of conquest to which a whole nation surrendered itself. But before surrendering to the passions of war the ideals of Christ were first forsaken by our enemy. A new law was promulgated: "Become hard, O my brethren, for we are emancipated and the world belongs to us." New beatitudes were declared: "Ye have heard how ... it was said, Blessed are the meek ... but I say unto you, Blessed are the valiant, for they shall make the earth their throne ... Ye have read, Blessed are the peacemakers, but I say unto you, Blessed are the war-makers, for they shall be called, if not the children of Jehovah, the children of Odin, who is greater than Jehovah."

Out of this new gospel, the gospel of Odin, has sprung a war of extermination—exiled nations, devastated kingdoms, desolated colleges, ruined cathedrals, and multitudes of women and children "left nothing but their eyes to weep with." The name of God has been invoked over unspeakable barbarities—but the God thus invoked is not the Christian God. It is Odin in whose name these things are done. What we are fighting for is for the Christian ideal against Odin—for the law of truth and mercy against the reign of falsehood of word and bond, and of merciless barbarity. We have bared the breast to death that there may sit on the throne of the world's soul, not a ruthless tribal god, but the God of Fatherhood and Love whom Jesus Christ revealed. And in waging that war we have ground to hope that the God of righteousness is on our side.

If we have not had the name of God constantly on our lips it is not because we do not feel that we are fighting His battle, but because He is so great, the Lord of Heaven and Earth before whom we are but as dust, that we shrink from coupling His great name with ours. "Are you sure that God is on your side?" Abraham Lincoln was asked in the dark days of the American Civil War. "I have not thought about that," he replied; "but I am very anxious to know whether we are on God's side." And when the causes of this war are examined the assurance grows stronger and stronger that we are on God's side. That is why the whole nation has been welded into the unity and consistency of polished steel; why the fire of patriotism burns in our midst with an intenser heat than ever before.

It is not merely from the righteousness of our cause in this war that our patriotism draws inspiration, but also from the ideals for which our Empire stands over all the world. As we look out to-day on the Empire which our fathers bequeathed us, taking it all in all, it stands for righteousness as no other on earth. It stands for the freedom of the soul and the freedom of the body all over the world.

Think of India, whose three hundred millions have been rescued from tyranny and ceaseless bloodshed, whose widows have been saved from the flames, whose starving have been fed in famine, and to whom the British race brought security and peace. "When I think," said ex-President Taft, "of what England has done in India ... how she found those many millions torn by internecine strife, disrupted with constant wars, unable to continue agriculture or the arts of peace, with inferior roads, tyranny, and oppression; and when I think what the Government of Great Britain is now doing for these alien races, the debt the world owes England ought to be acknowledged in no grudging manner."

No work ever done on earth for the elevation of humanity can compare with that wrought in India by our race for the uplift of humanity; and it is the same wherever the standard of Britain waves. In our own day we have seen in Egypt a whole race rising out of the mud and clothed anew in the garments of self-respect. Through Africa, wherever the sway of Britain extends, though yesterday the land reeked with blood, to-day mercy and kindness are healing the woes of men, and millions who knew not when death lurked for them in the bush now sleep in peace under the palms. It was the might of Britain that destroyed the slave trade, and it is nothing except the might of Britain which prevents the slave raider resuming his nefarious traffic, and slavery under the guise of other names being imposed on the natives of Africa. Wherever you go, to the tropics or the Orient, there the great power for righteousness is the British Empire. It does not exploit inferior races for gold; it is the trustee of the helpless native.

When one thinks of these little islands floating in the western sea, of the power that has gone forth from them to heal and bless, of the vast multitudes to whom the King-Emperor is the symbol of justice and security—his is a poor heart which cannot feel the thrill of gratitude for citizenship in an Empire girdling the whole earth, whose foundations are thus laid in righteousness.

Patriotism is not, however, a mere sentiment. It was not sentiment which built up the Empire. It was self-sacrifice—the spirit that faced and endured death. For us, too, patriotism must be more than sentiment; it must be action and the self-sacrifice which action requires.

What our fathers reared we must defend. And the startling thing is that there are still so many of our people who shrink from the burden which patriotism imposes. Many thousands refuse to prepare themselves for war; who are as the Romans who could not leave their baths to go and fight.

Vast multitudes congregate to gaze on football matches and gamble on the issue. The call of King and country falls on ears grown deaf. We thank God for those who, hearing the call, have gone forth to fight, counting everything but loss as compared to their country's gain. But these others, they cannot have paused to think. They have not pictured these fair lands, that have not heard the sound of war for seven generations, given over to that devouring enemy which has made Belgium a wilderness.

They have not thought of Oxford and St. Andrews sharing the fate of Louvain; of London and Edinburgh become as Brussels; of the millions of Glasgow and Birmingham thrown on the mercies of the world, women and children fleeing, driven by nameless fears, with no place to flee to but the mountain fastnesses of Wales and the Highlands of Scotland—the last refuge of the miserable and the broken. And yet these miseries would surely befall were all the manhood of the race such as these.

Think what it would mean were the walls of our defence broken down. Supposing that a shattering blow were struck at the heart of the Empire and our fleet crushed. What would follow? The crumbling of the Empire in a week! It is not we alone, with our wives and children in these little islands, who would be swept to ruin, and on whom despair would fall. From the far north-west to the long wash of the Australasian seas the shadow of devouring misery and death would fall on humanity. The millions of India would be forthwith swept into the whirlpools of war and mutiny. Egypt would be thrown back into chaos. Africa would be left to Islam and the merciless rule of a nation which knows but how to smite. Australia and New Zealand would be at the mercy of the yellow races.

It would not be a calamity for us in these islands alone. It would be a calamity whose withering blight would be cast over all the world. The ideals of righteousness which this Empire upholds would be trampled everywhere under foot. Covetousness and the lust of gold would hold the field of the world.

There is only one thing to be done, one duty summoning us with an irresistible call—the duty that calls us to stand between our country and destruction. Were the fate which has overtaken the Low Country to overtake us; were this fair land to be made a wilderness, our women and children driven into the wilds, and the Empire wrested from our hands, the men who failed in their duty would never be able to hold up their heads again.

What a terrible load would lie on him who, beholding the ruin of his native land, could say, "This might not have happened if I, and others like me, had done our duty." That would be a hell from which there would be no escape. "Which way I fly is hell; myself am hell."

There can be no limit to the sacrifice which patriotism requires, so great a heritage is our native land. It does not require of us as Christians to engage in wars of conquest for the gratification of pride and greed, but it does require of us even the sacrifice of our lives in the defence of our homes or in the defence of our brother's home.

There are those who find themselves faced with difficulty. They are called upon to fight with every force in their power, to slay, withholding not their hand, while they hear the commandment, "Thou shall not kill," ringing in their ears, and across the centuries the voice of their Lord saying, "Resist not evil; whosoever shall smite thee on the right cheek, turn to him the other also." They are bewildered. Is not the attitude of non-resistance that which Jesus Christ enjoins? If they fight with sword and shell are they not lowering themselves to the level of Nietzsche, Bernhardi and Bülow, and submitting to the arbitrament of the sword, which decides nothing except its own sharpness. The call of patriotism summoning to resist even unto blood comes to them, and they are uncertain whether to obey.

But we must interpret the will of God, not by isolated sentences, but by the whole content of the divine revelation. The commandment, "Thou shalt not kill," does not mean that we are not to kill in any circumstance whatever. If the commandment is to be taken literally, then no limit is to be set to it, and we must not kill any animal—not even the parasites of uncleanness. There is, moreover, another law which runs: "Whoso sheddeth man's blood, by man shall his blood be shed, for in the image of God created He him." So far from the mere physical life being for ever sacred, the very altar of God Himself was to be no sanctuary for the murderer. The man who owned a vicious ox and knew him to be vicious, and the ox killed a man, the owner thereof was to be slain. There are therefore circumstances in which the law, "Thou shalt not kill," is abrogated, and its place is taken by the law, "Thou shalt kill."

The law demanding the conservation of life rests on this foundation, not that physical life itself is sacred, but that human life bears the image of God. There are things far more sacred than the physical life—even those things which constitute the image of God stamped upon man. There are things for which men in all ages have been content to die—truth and loyalty to truth, the principles which are dearer than life. Those things which God ordained that men might through them grow more and more into His image, for these things man must be ready to die, and among these things is nationality.

Men cannot develop in isolation. What poor creatures men would be if they were solitary units. They would be as the beasts that perish. It is through the heritage of nationality that the soul is enriched. What poor stunted lives would ours be if we had not behind us the great and noble deeds which built up our Empire, if the words of the high souls of many generations did not come thrilling to our hearts, if Shakespeare and Wordsworth, Scott and Burns did not pour their treasures into our laps. The soul grows into the image of God through the riches of nationality. And whosoever warreth against nationality warreth against the soul. And the men who warreth against the soul must be resisted to the death.

We dare not appeal to Jesus Christ to cloak our shrinking from sacrifice. No doubt His gentleness has been the wonder of history; but His strength also summons us to be strong. For Jesus Christ was not a quietist. His religion is not a mere hospital for wounded souls. His place is among the strong of the earth. He faced the evil of this earth unflinching in His resistance.

"Woe unto you Scribes and Pharisees, hypocrites" is His denunciation of the oppressor; "Go tell that fox" is His message to the tyrant. When we think of Him making the whips, and falling, with holy anger in His eyes, on those who desecrated the courts of the temple, overturning the tables of the money changers, we know that the ideal of non-resistance is not His.

No doubt He laid it down as the law for the individual that he should turn the other cheek; but He did not lay it down as a law that a man should turn another's cheek to the smiter. What the individual can do, the nation may not do. It no doubt is the duty of the Ruler to turn his own individual cheek to the insulter; it is not his duty to turn the cheeks of the millions over whom he rules to those who would smite them, committing their children to shame and their homes to devastation.

No doubt Jesus Christ enjoined the law of forgiveness, but it was not unconditional. "If he repent, forgive him," is His law, and until the wrongdoer repents and ceases from his evil, it would be immoral to forgive him. Duty demands that every means be used to bring the evildoer to repentance; for only so is there a chance of his soul being saved. It is manifest that Christianity is not a religion of non-resistance to evil, but the religion of Him who Himself resisted evil, and who resisted it even to the death.

Patriotism, therefore, demands that we resist even to the shedding of blood. When a hostile army would destroy a nation, as in Belgium, it warreth against the soul, and it is as Christian to kill as it would be to shoot a tiger which leapeth out of the jungle to devour a man. And that Irish soldier whose face in the hospital in Paris was irradiated with joy when he was told that the enemy was put to flight and Paris saved, and who died with that gladness in his face, died in the spirit of Jesus Christ.

To say that the Founder of Christianity would not strike a blow for home and kindred and truth is to forget that He struck a blow in Jerusalem and wielded the thongs on the shoulders of those who polluted His Father's house. It is His will that we should strike a blow in defence of the house of our soul—the sanctuary of nationality.

Patriotism must be vibrant with the spirit of religion if it is to be a power rousing the nation to heroism and self-sacrifice. There never was a nation so patriotic as the Jew. No city ever gripped a nation's heart-strings as Jerusalem gripped the heart of the Jew. No suffering, no defeat, no exile however far, could quench the fire of patriotism in the heart. "If I forget thee, O Jerusalem, let my right hand forget her cunning. Let my tongue cleave to the roof of my mouth if I remember thee not, if I prefer not Jerusalem above my chief joy"—such was the cry of the Jew by the rivers of Babylon, yearning after Sion.

How was it that Jerusalem thus pulled at its children's heart-strings until they hurried back to rebuild? It was because Jerusalem was the seat of the worship of God. It was not the material stones or the hills round about that thus compelled the heart. It was the light of eternity shining over them. It was because of the "house of the Lord our God" that the Jew counted no good worth his striving except the good of Jerusalem. It is only when God standeth at the heart of a nation that the heart cleaveth with all its fibres to its native land, for then the whole of the man—not only the cravings of the body and the heart and the mind, but also the deeper cravings of the soul—wind themselves round the thought of the nation.

Thus we find that the days when the fires of patriotism burned brightest were ever those in which God held sway over the nation. It was with God that the sailors of Queen Elizabeth swept the main, that the soldiers of Wellington hurled the enemy far from the shores that face England—they were fighting not only for England but for England's God.

The testimony of history is this, that patriotism cannot maintain its power if once it be divorced from religion. Let God's face be veiled and lost and everything is lost. "Without God nothing, with God everything," says the ancient Celtic proverb, and all ages testify to its truth. And the last proof of it is now before our eyes in the condition of France.

A hundred years ago France dominated Europe, erected thrones and deposed kings at its will. But little by little France lost the vision of God, until at last M. Viviani celebrated the final triumph over the Church in 1907 by exclaiming: "With one magnificent gesture we have extinguished the lights of heaven, which none shall rekindle." France, in the words of its present Prime Minister, "extinguished the lights of heaven," but in so doing it extinguished something else. For to-day that nation, that not so long ago dominated Europe, can only protect its capital city by the help of the two nations which have not yet extinguished the lights of heaven.

Without God patriotism becomes impotent, for God is the source of that moral law, conformity to which means for a nation life, and defiance of which means the degeneration that leadeth to destruction. With the departure from God came moral decay and racial suicide. The hope of France is this, that through the descent of the nation into the valley of death the lights of heaven may be once more kindled; the hope of Britain, that these same lights may shine more brightly.

The spirit of patriotism will again vivify the nation when we seek after God. In years of prosperity we have forgotten our high calling. We have pursued vanities and forgotten the living God. When we again realise our calling and our election as instruments in the hand of God for the establishment of His Kingdom of Righteousness over all the earth, our hearts will be filled with ardour, and we shall face whatever perils may assail us strong in the assurance that the Omnipotent God is in our midst and that nothing can resist His will.

And this true patriotism will mean the salvation of the nation. For it will strive to realise at home that righteousness which alone exalteth a nation. Its first task will be to raise the life at home nearer to God, for we cannot raise the world to higher levels than that on which we ourselves stand. The vision of the new Jerusalem descending from God out of heaven will again flame before our eyes. "And I, John, saw the holy city, new Jerusalem, coming down from God out of heaven, prepared as a bride for her husband."

That new Jerusalem is not a city remote in the inaccessible heights, but a city which descends and permeates the material city now so polluted by sin, until it becomes the "holy city," with the law of God obeyed and the will of God done in it. Its citizens shall walk its streets, pure in heart, seeing God everywhere. "And they shall bring the glory and the honour of the nations into it." There the nations shall be one in the streets of the city of God, all their contendings forgotten in the sense of their brotherhood, following the one ideal, obeying the one law, loving each other in the love of God. They will strive then as to who shall bring the greatest glory within the compass of its walls, and that will be the only striving.

That is the ideal, that we should become a nation so permeated by the spirit of God, so brought into obedience to His will, that our cities shall become holy cities, even as the new Jerusalem coming down from God out of heaven. When we shall set ourselves to realise that ideal once more, then will the nation evoke the devotion of its citizens, for devotion to the nation will also be devotion to God.

It was that ideal which fired the patriotism of the Jew. The same ideal alone will make our patriotism glow as a white flame. When the vision of the Supreme Ruler whose throne is established in righteousness once more blazes forth before the people, then once more the throb of patriotism and the passion to make righteous law operative to the ends of the earth will stir the heart, and the manhood of the race will once more thrill with the call summoning to service and to sacrifice. The answering shout will everywhere arise—For God and the King.

# III
# The Shadow of the Cross

The churchyard of our parish lies in a deep hollow, and a little river half encircles it. In the midst of it stands the church beneath whose shadow the parish has garnered its dead for centuries. There the generations have lain down to sleep, their hearts reconciled one to another, and the beadle has drawn the coverlet of green over them. As he goes about his allotted task he pats a mound here and there gently with the back of his spade—for roadman and belted earl are at one here.

The last time I wandered down to the hollow it seemed as if eternal peace brooded over the living and the dead. The leaves, russet and gold, glowed in the sunlight. At the stirring of a gentle breeze, like the dropping of a sea-bird's feather, leaf after leaf fluttered silently down on the graves. The great bank of trees across the river glowed with rivulets of dull flames running hither and thither. In its stony bed the river sang its endless song. The immemorial yews, beneath whose branches successive generations of children have played with now and then a thrill of pleasing terror because of the overhanging graves, stood regardless of the sun. The crows, sated with the gleanings of harvest fields, fluttered in their rookeries with scarcely a caw. It seemed as if no sound of discord or strife could ever break in that enchanted hollow.

As I turned away to retrace my steps through the gate I came on a woman sitting on the mort-safe, a handkerchief moist with her tears in her hand. She had come up from the quarries and she had visited her dead. And she came because yesterday she received word that on the battlefield of Marne her son was killed. He was her eldest. The others were not old enough yet to fight. Her husband was killed in an accident, and she had reared her children, refusing all help from the parish. The pride of the blood sustained her. And now that her son was dead she came hither, driven by an irresistible instinct to visit her husband's grave. It was as if she wanted to tell him about John, and how he died a hero, trying to carry a wounded comrade through the hail of the shrapnel.

She was weary, and from her husband's grave she turned to the church. She would go and sit in the corner under the gallery, where John used to sit. He had sat with her there at his first Communion. The memories wrapped her round, and she would feel her son near her there. But the door of the church was locked and barred. With an added ache in her heart she turned away, and weariness compelled her to sit on the iron mort-safe, which the parish provided in a former century to protect their dead from sacrilegious hands. "But the church used to be open," I said. "Aye," she replied tremulously, gathering up her handkerchief into a round ball; "but some did-na like it; the boots on the week-days are na sae clean, and they dirtied the kirk. That must be why they lockit the door." It was not that she complained. Those who locked the church were wise men, and no doubt they knew best. So she sat on the mort-safe.

"I have other sons, and when they are older they will go, too," she said. "I'll no' keep them back. And if they die it'll be for God's great cause." Her lips quivered as she spoke. The moist ball in the right hand was clenched tight—there were no more tears to shed.

And as I looked at the worn, lined face, the bent shoulders, the faded rusty black mantle with its fringe, and the sunken lips that quivered now and then, there came a sudden realisation. I saw no longer the one grief-burdened figure sitting dejectedly on the mort-safe—I saw the unnumbered host of mothers throughout the world who have given their sons over to carnage, and who are as Rachel weeping for her children, refusing to be comforted because they are not. Millions of men locked in the death grapple means millions of mothers given tears to drink in great measure, bound in affliction and iron.

The song of the river went on ceaselessly, the russet-leaves fell softly, and the sun shone on a world wrapped in peace—all nature utterly regardless of the millions of Rachels that weep. (Ten million hearts may break, but nature silences not one note of its joyousness.) And as she sat there, behind her, under the campanile, showed the church door, locked and barred. Nature was heedless of her; the church shut its door upon her. She seemed to me the Mater Dolorosa.

As I went up the brae there came the memory of a school lesson long ago. Out of the subconscious it leaped as a diver might come up from the depths of the sea with a gleaming coin in his hand. Among the temples of ancient Rome there was one temple always kept open in time of war. There the Roman General clashed the shield and the spear, invoking the god ere he went to the battle-line, and its door was shut not day or night. And I have no doubt but that the Eternal Ruler heard that clashing of spear on shield, and marked that open door. But over wide districts of Great Britain we have left these pagan habits far behind us. We shut the doors of our temples alike in war and in peace—excepting two hours on one day of the week, or in many cases one hour in the week. Nor do I doubt but that the same Ruler marks these doors now shut on the mothers of sorrow, and these sanctuaries locked and silent.

The glory was now gone from the day. I could not forget how the iron mort-safe gave the rest that the Church refused. The shadow lay heavy over the valley, and the mind tried to give the shadow a name. But it could not. So up the long flight of stone steps I climbed, and turned along a tree-shaded road. There, where three roads meet, stands a little chapel within whose walls a small section of our parishioners worship. I have passed it times out of mind without so much as glancing at it. But to-day its open door arrested my eye, and I stood in the roadway and gazed. And there came to me there a sudden sense of thankfulness for that there is one open door in our parish which witnesses to the fact that the power and solace of religion are not shut in within the confines of only two hours of one day in the week.

While I yet stood in the highway there came forth from the little chapel an honoured parishioner, who is passing the golden evening of a useful life in researches regarding Calvin and the Pope. Amazement possessed me, for he is a power in the parish church, whose door is locked and barred. We walked together towards the hills. There was a trace of apology in his explanation. Since this dreadful cataclysm has burst and the boom of the guns has come drifting from the sea across the high-perched city, he has felt the need of quiet meditation. Thus he has often on his walks slipped through the open door of the chapel that stands by the roadside.

"And you have locked the door of the parish church," I exclaimed, "and you deny to the poor the privilege you yourself enjoy." He stopped and faced me in the roadway, blinking at me. "We never locked the Church door," he said. "It used to be open," I answered; "I remember being glad to sit in it myself." "Oh! I remember," he exclaimed, "it was open every day for a few years, but the authorities were never consulted when it was thrown open—a most lawless proceeding!—and when a suitable opportunity occurred the beadle locked it up. Law and order have to be vindicated."

"What you did then," I replied, "was to allow the beadle to deprive the poor parishioners of a privilege which you and a few others enjoy elsewhere." At that he started off walking along the road very quickly, but I kept step with him. "You see," said he, waving a deprecatory hand, "I am only one among many, and I was so absorbed in these old Reformation controversies that I never gave it a thought, and it is only since the war began that I realised...." And as he spoke I felt that my old friend, learned in many controversies, had experienced a revolution. The great tide had swept him past all controversies right up to the fountain head. He had learned that man's high calling is not to dispute, but to pray.

As we walked under the darkling hills I told him of that shadow which had so suddenly fallen upon me that day, and he at once gave it a name. "It is the shadow of the Cross," said he. And thereupon he began to explain out of the wisdom and ripened experience of seventy years how across nineteen centuries the shadow of the Cross lies still over all the world. One thinks so seldom of these things, and if occasionally one hears them spoken of, familiarity with the words has deadened the hearer to their significance. It was because I listened to him talking in the lane that his words gripped me. They might have made no impression if he were in a pulpit.

We are accustomed to think of the greatest of all tragedies as an event consummated in six hours. It is, however, far from consummated, for it is an age-long tragedy. Its roots lay in self-interest. A degenerate priesthood in an obscure Syrian town saw nothing in the Greatest of Teachers but an unbalanced enthusiast, who struck at their ill-gotten gains, and whose triumph would make an end of them and their system. So self-interest cried "Crucify." And though the Roman Governor saw through them and wanted to save Him, self-interest again was brought into play, and when threatened with an awkward complaint to Rome, he said "Crucify." And ever since then self-interest on innumerable lips has cried Crucify, Crucify. Not only cried, but did it.

For this Teacher identified Himself with His followers, saying that He was the Vine and they the branches. It follows that whatever is done to the branch is done to the vine. A branch cannot be cut and severed from the vine without the vine bleeding. He declared it to be so. "Whosoever receiveth you receiveth Me," and it follows that whosoever crucifies you crucifies Me. And the history of the centuries is the history of how the poor and unlearned and the toiling have been persecuted, harried by war, driven to death and crucified.

Generation after generation have raised the Cross anew, and in the crucifying of the dumb multitudes have crucified Him. Along with His own He fought with wild beasts, went through the flames, and suffered many bloody and diverse persecutions, and He was with His people now. He confronted to-day the mighty of the earth as He did that blinded priesthood of old, and He declared that there is only one way of conquering, and that by love; that gaining the whole world was a miserable bargain if in exchange a man parted with truth and righteousness and purity—those things that constitute the soul's very breath.

But self-interest answered with cold disdain: "What sickly sentimentalist is this? Let Him be crucified." He faced to-day the lust of conquest, and declared that the conquering of men's bodies was nothing; that the only way of attaining power was to conquer men's hearts and minds and wills, thus clasping them to us with hooks of steel; that the will of God for His children was that they should love their enemies and not pour upon them the vials of wrath, trampling them under foot; but the arrogance of man answered with the hoarse cry, "Crucify."

And that humanity which named His name was driven once more to the holocaust of war—ten millions of men consigned to the hell of reeking trenches. In the midst of the world the Cross stands as never before, bearing its awful woe. In the seeing of the whole world the Eternal Love is crucified. It was its shadow that fell on her whose lips trembled as she sat on the mort-safe over against the locked and barred door of the House of God.

The most wonderful thing in history is that from a peasant done shamefully to death in a remote corner of the Eastern world there should flow through the ages such an inexplicable power. And yet there must be some explanation of it. Why should a passion for righteousness be evoked in the human heart by the fact that a Galilean was crucified by a petty Roman official? There can be no explanation but this—that that deed of shame revealed to men the hatefulness of the power which wrought so evil a deed. That power was self-interest—selfishness.

The eyes of men turned to Jesus Christ, and they saw one holy, harmless, undefiled, separate from sin, whose journeying was the journeys of healing among the sons of men, whose words were words of blessedness, declaring that God loved and pardoned His children, and yet men reviled, scorned, scourged and at last crucified Him. The power that moved men to this dread crime was sin, and thus the word sin became a word of horror. (For the selfishness that crucified was only one fruit of sin.) Out of that realisation of the horror of sin there sprang an ethical passion—a passion which in the heart and in the world waged ceaseless war on selfishness and all the devices of evil. Thus humanity was lifted out of the mire. They girded themselves to fight that dread and hateful power which crucified the Holy One.

Like the wind blowing in from the sea that sweeps before it the foul miasma that lies over the valleys, so that men look up and see the heavens and feel a new vigour moving in their blood, so a breath from the living God came stirring the foul places of humanity, and the eyes, no longer blinded by the exhalations of evil passions, saw the ideal of purity arise before their eyes, and they turned to climb towards the clearer vision. Through the revelation of purity in the face of Jesus Christ and the realisation of the awfulness of that power which crowned that purity with thorns, there came to humanity the dawning of deliverance from sin—a deliverance still going on to its fruition.

History is for ever repeating itself, and to-day the process of humanity's deliverance from evil will gather momentum and advance a long way towards the final triumph. For just as men only realised the hatefulness of sin when they saw it laid upon Jesus Christ, so will it be also to-day. A generation that had lost the sense of sin beholds sin laid upon millions of men, working woe unspeakable, and, beholding, learns anew what sin is and the hatefulness of it. For these millions of men grappling with death, what are they but humanity's sin-bearers. On them is laid the burden of the sins of this generation. The selfishness, greed, ambition, lust—all the passions which sweep men to wars of conquest—have poured the vials of misery on their heads. The son of the widow sitting on the mort-safe, who now lies in a nameless grave, he bore it. The bearing of it killed him.

And as humanity will realise its horror, the word sin will once more burn red before men's eyes, and there will arise that passion for righteousness which will lay sin low even as the dust. There will ring round the world the compelling cry that this power of hell must not for ever hold humanity in its grip—that ruthless ambition, militarism, despotism must be made to cease from the face of the earth. Once more the shadow of the Cross will mean salvation to men.

There was another power also that stirred the world under the shadow of the Cross, and that was the power of self-sacrifice. There came to men an overwhelming realisation that at the heart of the universe was the Spirit of self-sacrifice, and that the Cross was but the expression of it. They realised that the greatest thing a man can do with his life is to lay it down. And as men realise to-day that the Cross still abides in the heart of God, so that in all their affliction He is afflicted, there comes to them the feeling that the one way of coming nearest to His heart is the way of self-sacrifice.

Under the shadow of the Cross now lifted up, a nation that sought life's pleasures has suddenly thrilled with the glory of self-sacrifice. What is it that sustains the men who go down to the earthly hell of ruthless war? It is just this—the consciousness, newly wakened, of how glorious a thing it is to die for King and country, for home and kindred. They are content to be blotted out if only the race will live, to descend to the abyss that the nation may be exalted. Under the shadow of the Cross self-sacrifice has become once more the only rock on which our feet can stand secure. Men charge across fields of death with the light of it in their eyes. They are raised into the fellowship of the Cross. And we are raised with them.

If I could only tell the bowed widow sitting there on the mort-safe the glorious fellowship with which her son is numbered, she would again lift up her face to the light. He has died that we may live. Greater love hath no man than this—nor yet greater glory. But she needs not to be told; she knows it already. She knows it far better than you or I do, for she feels it. In the deep places of life where words are meaningless, her dumb heart feels the mystery of sin-bearing and the glory of self-sacrifice.

By a faculty deeper and truer far than reason, in the depths of the soul where the Unseen Spirit moves revealing the things that are of lasting worth, she has learned in meekness and suffering that divine wisdom which is hid from the wise. She knows that the road that goes by Calvary up to the Cross is the one road along which the feet can come to God. She knows that her son has walked along that road, and that, because of his bearing the cross laid upon him, and his dying while bearing it, God has brought him into that joy which all the cross-bearers see shining beyond the darkness and the woe. And because she has thus entered into the secret place of the Most High, and has felt the touch of God, she is ready to greet the day of still greater sacrifice.

In the evening, when the curtains were drawn, I took up a magazine and read an article. It was a bitter invective against Christianity and the Church. Nineteen centuries of the religion of the Cross—and this holocaust as the fruit. It is amazing the blindness of the jaundiced eye. It would be as reasonable to blame the Founder of Christianity for His own crucifixion as to blame Christianity for the fact that the wicked have continued to crucify Him. These things are so not because, but in spite, of Christianity.

Grievous as war now is, yet it is not war as in the days before the Cross was erected on Calvary. When Ulysses asked Agamemnon for sanction to bury the body of Ajax, the King was greatly annoyed. "What do you mean?" he answered, "do you feel pity for a dead enemy?" That was the spirit of war in the old heathen world—the spirit which had no mercy on the living and no pity for the dead. Slowly but surely the spirit of Christ fettered the spirit of hate and dethroned the spirit of revenge. We now minister to the wounded and bury the dead enemy with the pity and the honour we render to our own.

We can trace the evolution of peace through the centuries. Wars between individuals have ceased. A century and a half ago warring clans in Scotland dyed the heather red; to-day wars between tribes have ceased.

There remains only war between nations, and already there are great nations between whom war is unthinkable. If we in these days wage war with Germany, yet we in these days also celebrate the hundredth anniversary of unbroken peace with the United States of America. If we bewail the failure of Christianity in the former, let us be grateful for the triumph of Christianity in the latter.

Formerly war was the normal condition; now to the moral consciousness of Christendom war is an outrage. We only need to look beneath the surface to realise that Galilee is conquering Corsica, and will conquer at the last. Beneath the shadow of the Cross men will at last find healing for their grievous wounds.

And as a symbol thereof the doors of the sanctuaries of peace will be flung wide open, and no burdened heart will find the House of God locked and barred against groping hands. One fruit of these grievous days may well be that the Church will realise that it does not become her to occupy a lower plane than that heathen temple in ancient Rome, whose door was shut not day or night while men were dying in battle.

In the coming days when the mothers of sorrow come to their dead, over whose graves the falling leaves flutter as a benediction, they will not be left sitting on the iron mort-safe. The open door will invite them into the sanctuary of peace, and they will croon the coronach of their woe in the holy place. For they are the priesthood of this generation, offering up the most precious sacrifice—and the door of the holy place must be open to them. And there, in the sanctuaries of peace, their sorrow will be transmuted into joy.

# IV
# The Power of Prayer

For eight centuries the Church of St. Giles has been the centre of the religious life of Scotland. At all times of sorrow the nation has turned to it, and within its walls, consecrated by the prayers of so many generations, the surcharged heart has voiced its woe in the presence of the Unseen. But in all the years of the dim and fading past there never was a day like this in which we now stand. Death has come as a grim spectre, and has looked into our eyes. The winds carry to our ears the moans of our perishing sons, dying gloriously for freedom on the bloody fields of Flanders. The great ships guard our shores, and we know that if that vigil failed, our cities and villages and fair countryside would become as Louvain and the Low Country. Death itself would be welcome rather than that.

If there ever came to any nation a call to seek the refuge which eye has not seen, that call soundeth persistently, compellingly in our ears. And that call soundeth not in vain. To-day[1] the two great Churches of Scotland met as one in St. Giles, the days of their misunderstanding ended, to pray for King and country—for all the things which make life beautiful. They have come through days of alienation and isolation, but to-day they are with one accord in one place. And in their hearts only one purpose—to seek the blessing of God for their nation.

[1] November 18, 1914.

As one sat there, under the tattered flags on which many bloody fights for freedom are emblazoned, and watched the stream of men flow into the church, what memories came crowding through the echoing corridors of time.

Four hundred years ago there came to Edinburgh the news of Flodden, and out of the closes the women rushed to St. Giles, until round all the altars there was no room to kneel because of the great crowd wailing for their dead. The moaning of their lamentation was as the sound of the surf wailing on the shore, and their sobbing as the cry of the grinding pebbles in the backwash of the tide. But the city fathers could stand upright even in that most cruel day when the cloud of destruction was creeping over the

Pentlands; and there is the note of the heroic in that resolution which called all the able-bodied men to rally to the defence of the capital, and exhorted "the good women to pass to the kyrk, and pray whane tyme requires for our Soveraine Lord and his Army, and neichbouris being thereat."

That proclamation stirs the blood! They are dust, these fathers of ours, but their spirit is all alive, throbbing in the heart of us—their far-away children. Never did a race meet its Sedan in a sublimer spirit than that. The strong, at toll of bell and tuck of drum, manned the ramparts, and the women filled St. Giles' and sent heavenward their cries. The bodies of such a race may for a brief season be brought to subjection, but their souls are invincible—and it is the soul that always conquers.

And here to-day it is the same. From every part of Scotland men have come, and they passed "to the kirk to pray for our Sovereign Lord and his Army." True, there has been no Flodden and no Sedan; but it is by the good hand of God upon us that the enemy was frustrated in his eagerness for another Sedan. And it is in part the prayer of thanksgiving that is laid to-day upon His altar, and in part the petition that His mercies may be continued to the nation in the cruel days to come.

What a sanctuary for a nation's prayers, this church, where Kings have prayed and gone forth to die in battle; where Queens have wept as the voice of judgment, grim and stern, untouched by tenderness or love, sounded in the ear; where three thousand people dissolved in tears as the good Regent, foully slain, was borne to his grave. Over it passed wave after wave of fanaticism and barbarism; and at last it fell into the hands of the restorers— more ruthless far than Goths or Vandals! But, through it all, the house of God survived; and, apparelled once more in some of its pristine glory, it opens its doors to a nation that once more seek after its God.

And above us, as we sit there, hang the colours of our Scottish regiments stirring our patriotism, assuring us that the men who guarded these flags on many bloody fields were guarded by God, and that we are still in His keeping.

What a place this is in which to set vibrating that note of patriotism which now quivers from Maiden Kirk to John o' Groat's. These colours there—they are the most eloquent things on earth, for they pertain to the realm of symbols. Words are poor compared to tears, and that is because tears belong to the world of symbols. That tattered banner there belonged to the Gordon Highlanders, and was carried through the Peninsula and the Crimea. Woven in faded letters you can read on it still Corunna, Almarez, Pyrenees, Waterloo. Ah! these flags tell of a devotion stronger than death, rekindle the memories of the day when stern silence fell on the ranks, as the

Highland Brigade breasted the slopes of the Alma until Sir Colin Campbell lifted his hat and they rushed on the foe with the slogan of victory; and that other day when "the thin red line tipped with steel" rolled back the surge of the Cossacks; aye, and of a hundred such days when men went down joyously to death that the race might be free and live.

Waterloo!—it is on many flags. And we remember how the Man of Destiny himself, as he saw his ranks yield before the onslaught of the Highlanders, did not restrain his admiration for his enemies, but exclaimed with the true soldier's generosity, "Les braves Ecossais"—"Brave, brave Scotsmen" (what a contrast to "French's contemptible little Army"). The hands that carried, the hearts that thrilled at the waving of these flags, their fame will never perish.

"On the slopes of Quatre Bras
The Frenchmen saw them stand unbroken.
*  *  *  *  *


On the day of Waterloo
The pibroch blew where fire was hottest.
*  *  *  *  *


When the Alma heights were stormed
Foremost went the Highland bonnets.
*  *  *  *  *


As it was in days of yore,
So the story shall be ever.
*  *  *  *  *
                   .

Think then of the name ye bear,
Ye that wear the Highland tartan.
*  *  *  *  *


Zealous of its old renown,
Hand it down without a blemish."

As the eye looks along the nave up into the choir and sees the gleam of red, colours after colours, there comes the memory of words—"We have heard with our ears, O God, and our fathers have told us what work Thou didst in their days in the times of old.... Through Thee will we push down our enemies...." The unseen God who has led His people through so many and great dangers will not forsake them now.

There is a tablet where formerly stood the door that led to Haddo's Hole, and there hangs on a pillar the flag that pertains of truth to the realm of romance. Men with their hearts hot with indignation buried it in Pretoria in 1880, and put above it the inscription "Resurgam." Afterwards the Colonel recovered it and brought it home. When war broke out again his widow restored it to the regiment—the Royal Scots Fusiliers. In 1881 that regiment was the last to leave the Transvaal; in 1900 it was the first to enter the Transvaal—as the inscription narrates. And by the direction of Lord Roberts, when Pretoria was occupied, this identical flag was run up amid the shouts of the victors. Now it rests here. "Resurgam"—it is the unquenchable spirit of an invincible nation.

If only the manhood of Scotland could be gathered into this Church, under these flags, and the story they tell were put into words, pulsating with passion—then the ranks of our Army would be filled up in a week. What a lack of imagination we reveal! We teach dates, thinking we are teaching history. The only way to teach history is by flags, and all they stand for. When Douglas threw the heart of Bruce among his enemies he cried, "Lead thou on as thou wast wont and Douglas will follow thee or die." In the spirit of Douglas our fathers followed the flags, and we will follow in the steps of our fathers and face death with undaunted hearts as they were wont. There comes to us the shouting of their triumph, and we cry: "Lead on; we will follow or die." This grey church, St. Giles', is the temple of patriotism. Therefore our feet turn towards it in dark days, and we say, "Our feet shall stand within thy gates, O Jerusalem!"

How the old words are born for us anew as we thus meet as one "to entreat God for the broken peace of Christendom." We sing "God is our refuge and our strength," but there is a note of intensity in the singing now such as we never knew before. Men close their eyes, and stand, the world blotted out, before their God, realising that He and He alone is the one refuge, the only giver of victory. We hear the old story read of Moses holding up his hands and Israel prevailing on the plains below; but it is not Israel we see travailing in battle, but our own brothers in the rain-sodden trenches, and we feel the uprising of the ceaseless intercession of a nation that has anew found its God. It is not the right hand that assureth victories; it is that spirit of enthusiasm, that passion for righteousness which filleth the heart, and that spirit is as the wind blowing where it listeth—and it cometh out of the Unseen at the call of our prayers.

When in other days we prayed for the King it was in the spirit of cold formalism. But now a lump rises in the throat as we invoke the blessing and protection of Heaven for the solitary man who is the symbol of the unity of our Empire, and who watcheth over its destinies day and night, and who has sent his son to face death with the meanest of his subjects. We hear the glorious words: "If God be for us, who can be against us?" and they are written for ourselves. We, who fight for the truth of word and for the freedom and deliverance of the oppressed, can feel that God is for us, and that all is well.

And when we pray, our voices rising as one, "Thy kingdom come," we can see that kingdom coming through blood and tears, cleansing the foul places and establishing peace on everlasting foundations. It is a new day that has dawned for us—a day in which we stand united as the subjects of the one King, as the sons of the one God—and the things that separated us one from another are swept away. What the conferring of the wise found so difficult to achieve, the roaring of the guns has accomplished. God teacheth his people by sending them through the purifying fires.

In these prayers in St. Giles' there is a directness which shows that we are there for a definite purpose. We no longer use qualifying words. We cry for victory. There is a bloodless form of prayer which some use and which sends the worshipper away with an aching heart. It is the prayer that never prays directly for victory. "Thy will be done," it prays, in the spirit of submission. But prayer is not submission; it is a wrestling. In other days our fathers wrestled in prayer and prevailed. "I spent the night in prayer," wrote Oliver Cromwell, in critical days; "I prayed God that He would guide us against the enemy. We were simple fellows of the country, and they were men of blood and fashion, but the Lord delivered them into our hands. By His grace we killed five thousand. If He continues to show mercy we will kill some more to-morrow." Such were the Ironsides, "men of a spirit," who broke the charges of the Cavaliers, as the cliff dashes back in white spray the rush of the billows.

This was also the language of the Covenanters of old; and though we no longer use such plainness of speech, we mean the same. There is a place for tenderness; but when men are ground to powder by the judgment of God, tenderness is not manifest then. When the heart whispers "Spare" and justice says "Smite," men must obey the voice of justice, stifling the voice of the heart.

Our prayers are now for justice. Better far a righteous war than an immoral peace. We have been compelled to unsheath the sword, and we pray that no heart may falter, and no cry arise for the sheathing of the sword, until justice be done. Thus our prayers have become a cry for victory.

As one sits in an ancient church such as this, there comes knocking at the heart many questions regarding that service of prayer which within its walls has linked the generations together. Can prayer really prevail with

God? Can it alter the will of the Unchangeable? If there be no power in it, why should men go on praying?

We must distinguish between the will of God which is unchangeable, and His lower will which is his purpose towards us and His attitude to us. The former is unalterable; the latter varies according to the varying of our hearts. With that lower will we are called to wrestle. A man is born in poverty and obscurity, and the will of God seems to be that he should continue poor and obscure. But he wrestles with that lower will until he prevails. He ultimately moves out into the great tide of life and becomes a power. The will of God towards that man is changed.

It is the same with a nation. Here is a nation sinking on its lees with its ideals dimmed and the shrines of its fathers' God forsaken and desolate. It has fashioned to itself other gods, and the multitudes crowd the temples of the goddess of pleasure. The very race itself is sacrificed on the altar of gross pleasure, and the laughter of little children is being little by little silenced. The fires of patriotism are dying low, and the love of country gives place to the love of party. There are mean victories rejoiced over, but they are the victories of the cynic and the sensualist. There is the sound of shouting, but it is the shouting over the triumph of one self-seeking politician over another self-seeking partisan. Saintliness, which other generations held in awe and reverence, provokes now a pitying smile. Mammon alone is held in high honour and sitteth in the high places. What is the will of God towards that nation? It is this—ruin and utter destruction. Over every nation that thus succumbed to the gross and sensual, history shows the sword of God unsheathed, and at last the devouring flames of judgment.

But to such a nation there comes as if out of the silent heaven a call as a trumpet sound, summoning it to the judgment-seat of God. Over the sea comes the roar of guns. The foundations which the fathers laid in righteousness, through long neglect and decay are crumbling. An empire encircling the globe is tottering to destruction. The hay and the stubble cannot come scathless through the flames. The writing is on the wall, and as the eyes see the hand that writes, trembling seizeth upon men. And then there cometh a sudden change. The nation in a day rises out of the morass of its self-indulgence. It sets itself to lay hold again upon the eternal law of righteousness. They seek once more the shrines of their God. They set themselves to fast and to pray. "Who can tell," they whisper one to another, "if God will turn and repent, and turn away from His fierce anger, that we perish not?"

The fields of their inglorious shouting over their games are deserted for the fields of hardness and grim preparation. Once more they gird themselves for conflict, as their fathers so often girded, that truth and righteousness may prevail over all the earth. Sharply the choice is presented to them between Christ or Odin, and though choosing the Christ means agony and woe they make their choice unhesitatingly. A new light shines in their eyes, and the work of their hands and the devisings of their hearts become the spirit of prayer. Yesterday the will of God towards that nation, sinking on its lees, was destruction; to-day towards that same nation, thus risen out of the foul miasma that was stifling its soul, the will of God is salvation.

Because prayer is the greatest power in the world; because it can alter the will of God towards us, because it can move the hand of the omnipotent God and is thus endued with His omnipotence, our prayers as we gather in the sanctuaries are no longer the submission of quietism, but a wrestling with God—the crying of a soul as in agony for victory based on the triumph of righteousness. It was such a cry that rose on that day in St. Giles.

As the second paraphrase was being sung there came the memory of words spoken in the pulpit of the great Cathedral by Dr. Cameron Lees. It was at evening service, when the shadows were gathering. "I have often sat in this pulpit," said Dr. Lees, "on the edge of the evening, and watched the shadows enveloping the Cathedral. They invaded the side chapels first, and then the nave, creeping onwards through the transepts, until the chancel was reached. After that they gathered in strength, until the whole building was in darkness, with the exception of the white figure of Christ in the great east window. I pray that the last vision vouchsafed me on earth may be just that—the Saviour of men. I can then close my eyes in the knowledge that He will lead me through the dark valley that leadeth to the eternal home."

It has been like that with the whole nation. Around our shores the darkness gathered, until all the horizon was black with threatening clouds. Then we lifted up our eyes and saw.... He will bring deliverance and peace. As we moved along the crowded aisles towards the door the white figure of Christ glowed in the great east window, and we felt that He will bless His people at last with peace—the peace not of death, but of life.

> "Down the dark future, through long generations,
> The echoing sounds grow fainter and then cease,
> And, like a bell, with solemn sweet vibrations,
> I hear once more the voice of Christ say Peace.
> Peace! and no longer from its brazen portals
> The clash of war's great organ shakes the skies;
> But beautiful as songs of the immortals,
> The holy melodies of love arise."

# V
# The Victory

The blinds were all drawn in the red-roofed house that stands at the cross-roads. It was not empty, for the smoke arose from its chimneys in the clear morning air. In other days the music of song and laughter often floated from its open windows, but now it was stricken dumb. From it two sons had gone to take their place in the line of soul and fire that girdles these islands, warding them from destruction.

In a moment the veiled windows flashed their meaning. In the long lists of the dead I found the name I looked for. I had schooled myself to look at these lists, thinking of them in the mass as force or power; but that one name insisted on its individuality. They were all individual lives, each throbbing with intensest self-realisation, each with his love and hope and fear. There was none among them so poor but some heart clung to them. They may die, no longer in units, but in broad swathes, mown down by machine guns, but they are individual hearts still. In masses the sea swallows them up, trenches are filled with them, but however much we try we cannot narcotise our hearts by sophistries. Some day a name stands out alone—and we realise.

All over the land, in every parish, blinds are being drawn in houses where music and laughter are silenced. There comes the surge of a wild revolt. It is not these individual hearts alone that lie stricken, it is the joy of the centuries yet to be. In nameless graves lie the dream-children who will never now be born. This criminal sealing up of the very fountain of life— how can we bear it?

And yet we open not our mouths in protest. Is it because we are losing our sensitiveness—becoming brutalised? It might be that. For nothing coarsens the mind like that tide of hatred and passion which war sends sweeping through the hearts of men. And yet it is not that. For when they told the mother, breaking it gently as love alone can do, that her son was dead, she bowed her head in silence, yielding herself to the solace of tears; but in a little while she said brokenly: "It is good to die so: I would not have my son shelter himself behind other mothers' sons."

No, it is not because we are already coarsened that the heart can bear. It is rather because we have realised with the passing away of the old world of the last long summer days (it seems already centuries remote) that there are some things so great that they can transfigure even death. When the loyalty to the highest can only be fulfilled through death, we acquiesce in the sacrifice. In our parish we have not been coarsened—we have been quickened.

It seems as if it were in another era that my friend at the top of the Gallows' Road proved to me convincingly that death alone was king. With a keen irony he depicted this little globule of a world, a third-rate satellite of a fifth-rate star, floating in the abysses, in relation to the universe but as a mere grain of sand amid all the sand on the world's shores; and on that puny speck of a world he pictured the ephemeral generations, mere flashes of troubled consciousness—and then darkness.

It was reasonable when they thought this world the centre of all things, with the sun and moon and stars circling it round as humble ministrants, that they should believe in some high destiny for themselves. But now that they know how miserably and unspeakably insignificant the world is, it was but vanity and arrogance for any man to think of himself as of any value whatever in the scheme of things. His life was as the flashing of a midge's wings. His end was as a candle blown out in the night.

One evening, when the air was vibrant with the melody of birds and laden with the perfume of the roses that filled the garden, he developed another train of thought. He pictured the glut of life there would be if all the generations on this and millions unnumbered of worlds all survived. With vivid gestures he passed them all before the eye—low-browed savages, cannibals, fetish-worshippers, Calvinists, and at last the æsthetics of our day. "There would be no room for them—no use for them at all—it would be a glut which baffles all imagination." There was no way out but that the individual perished to prevent the universe from being crowded out.

And the cobbler at the top of the brae described to me how his dog was run over in the street. "He gaed a bark—and he never gaed anither. It'll be like that at the end with us a'. We'll gae out like my dawg." It was a queer result of the glimpse which came to us of an illimitable universe—this cheapening of ourselves. There was nothing at last but the charnel-house of the crowded kirkyard, where the generations lay layer upon layer, and where the opening of a grave reminded the old clerk, as he quaintly declared, of nothing but a dentist's shop. The teeth survived for unrecorded centuries—but that was all.

It is strange the tricks the memory plays. For, sitting here, glancing over the crowded sheet filled with the names of the dead, I remembered these things. And there came the sense of the madness of the universe and the intolerableness of life, if the end of all heroism was but that—nothingness and corruption. A handful of bones thrown up by the beadle to make room for the dead of to-day—is that all that is left of those who handed down the lamp of life to us? Is that all that will be left of us too at the last?

In the ordinary day my friend at the top of the Gallows' Road and the cobbler on the breast of the brae would have said that that was the end. But the extraordinary day has come upon us unawares, and in the extraordinary day this little, burdened, pain-racked life becomes suddenly unendurable unless it lie in the bosom of eternity. If there be no rainbow circling the heavens above the carnage heaps of the stricken battlefields, if the farewell of death be a farewell for ever, how can the heart endure?

It certainly looks to the seeing of the eye as if destruction were the end. With the perishing of the body everything seemeth to perish: all love, all thought, all tenderness vanish for ever. But the eyes and the ears are for ever playing us false; and here, too, they deceive us. For the world is so ordered that nothing ever perishes. In nature there is no destruction. A handful of ashes in a grate look like annihilation, but what it represents is really resurrection. The imprisoned sunrays of uncounted æons, stored up in the lumps of coal, have been released from the prison-house, and gone forth again as heat and as light. The physical body may seem to perish; what really happens is that its constituent elements are re-grouped.

But in the realm of beauty, is there not destruction possible there? Through long centuries faith and devotion rear a great cathedral, every line and curve of which is instinct with beauty. Every statue breathes the love and hope and fears of men. In vaulted aisles and "windows richly dight," it symbolises the Unseen—the beauty which the heart yearns for. On that beauty materialised, ruthless Vandalism rains shot and shell; the devouring flames consume it. Its gaunt walls are now a monument of barbarism. Has nothing perished there? Is it not mockery to speak of the conservation of the constituent elements there? For loveliness has vanished there from off the face of the earth, and beauty which no hand of man can ever restore has been annihilated.

But it has not. For beauty is not in things, but in souls. The beauty lay in the soul of the architects that planned, in the hearts of the builders that carved the stones until they seemed to breathe—and shells cannot destroy that. The loveliness was shrined in the souls of the generations that gazed, and, gazing, were raised into the fellowship of the hearts that planned and builded. Thus did the spirit of beauty grow in the hearts of men—and shells cannot destroy that.

And let these charred walls be left to the alchemy of time, and nature will clothe them in richer loveliness. Lichen and moss will grow on them, and the moonlight will etherialise them. One symbol of beauty may seem to perish; but the spirit of beauty itself, dwelling in the hearts of men and abiding at the core of the universe, is indestructible. The thing which we deem perishable, no power on earth can kill.

There is on earth something infinitely more precious than the material substance, indestructible though it be. The most beautiful thing the world can show is a good man. Through the years forces play on him, and each force adds its element of beauty. He has struggled with adversity, and in the conflict he has learned patience, tolerance and a wide charity. Waves of affliction have passed over him, and he has learned tenderness and sympathy with human suffering, so that bruised hearts come and lie down in his shadow, and there find healing. With eyes cleansed from self, he looks out on the comedy and tragedy of life, and he sees the hidden springs. The healing power that goes forth from him grows with the years. At last he dies.

Does nature conserve the shell while it consigns the jewel in the shell—the man himself, with all his love and tender thought and unselfish care—to annihilation? That is unthinkable. To know one good man is to know that the human personality is imperishable. It was through that knowledge that the soul of man triumphed over the terror of death.

There walked in Galilee a Teacher who made a handful of peasants feel the possibilities of moral loveliness latent in the human heart, and when He died they could not associate the thought of death with Him. "It was not possible that He should be holden of it," they said one to another. Everything was possible but that He could become as a clod in the valley of corruption. Of course even that was possible if the world were a chaos given over for sport to malicious demons.

It would be possible, then, that the self-sacrificing love stronger than death, and the spirit of unsullied purity should become mere dust. But the possibility of the world being ruled by any except a Righteous Power did not occur to the untutored Galileans. Therefore they faced death with level eyes, refusing to believe in its triumph, saying to their hearts, "It is not possible."

And that is the rock on which to plant our feet in the day when the world is given over to the wild welter of bloodshed. In every parish over all the land blinds are pulled down, and hearts, wrapped round in the dimness, sit still in the shadow of a dumb affliction. They will never again hear the familiar footsteps coming to the door; they will hear it in their dreams—only to awake and find silence. Never again will the first question be when the door is opened, as it was through all the days since the golden days of childhood, "Where is mother?" But the great things which made life noble have not been destroyed by bullet or shell. No man is worthy of freedom except the man who is prepared to die for it. The heart, which in death proved itself deserving of freedom, has entered into the fulness of freedom. The heavens are again aglow when we realise that.

It was the Professor who made me sure of those things. I met him at the "Priory," where my old friend carries on his controversy with the Pope—or used to. In that house of his one meets all sorts of visionaries from the ends of the earth. A Waldensian pastor full of the dream of a rejuvenated Italy; a leader of French Protestants, who has forgotten his controversy with the Pope in the great upheaval through which his race are finding their soul once more; a dreamer from across the Atlantic, his eyes a-gleam with the vision of a reunited Christendom—these are the men you will find drinking tea at the Priory on any day in our parish.

The original bond between them was their controversy with Rome, but they have now forgotten all about that. There, in a happy hour, I met the Professor. One phrase of his lit up for me the days of darkness. "We see the alchemy of Providence at work all round about us," he exclaimed, pushing his fingers through his hair until it stood up all on end, an aureole of white.

"It is the flower of our manhood that is perishing," said the "Prior," while our hostess was nervously solicitous over the fate of a teacup which the Professor was balancing in his left hand, utterly regardless of its purpose.

"Perishing!" exclaimed the Professor; "they are not perishing—they are living. To talk of the wastage of life is mere cant." Our hostess rescued the teacup, and the Professor had now the free use of both his hands. The one hand clutched his hair and the other made sundry gestures clinching his arguments.

"Why should we rail at death?" said he; "for death has been the saviour of humanity. It was death that made men of us. It was in the school of death that man learned unselfishness, self-sacrifice, chivalry and honour. There is nothing so ugly as the man whose heart is filled by the world. It is death that has saved us all from that. Were man's location here for ever, the world would be his god. A world without death would be a world with no room for the Cross. Men climbed the heights of nobility as they defied death. The crackling flames were unable to silence the martyrs' song; the march of the hosts of devouring tyranny could not move the hearts that chose death rather than slavery; the generations sealed with their blood their testimony that truth and loyalty to truth are more precious than life, and so met death with a smile; it was through this wrestling with death that great and noble character was forged on the anvil of life. Death was the weapon which forged greatness of soul. Death cannot destroy what death has created. That could only happen in an insensate world. What is it—death—but just this—the slave of immortality?"

If I could only write it down as the Professor spoke, if I could only make you see his eyes glowing with little darts of flame as he saw the whole world transformed into a mighty workshop in which the "alchemy of Providence" is transmuting the soiled substance of our humanity into living souls (over whom death can have no dominion) fashioned for heavenly destinies—then you, too, would believe. Since that day my old friend has not spoken a word about the "waste of the flower of the race."

The house with the drawn blinds stands at the cross-roads, and I must come back to it. What is it that has happened to him who lies in a nameless grave in France? The opportunity for winning glory and earthly fame did not come his way; he just laid down his life along with hundreds of thousands more. He has taken his place among the undistinguished dead.

> "O, undistinguished dead,
> Whom the bent covers or the rock-strewn steep
> Shows to the stars, for you I mourn—I weep,
> O, undistinguished dead.
>
> "None knows your name,
> Blackened and blurred in the wild battle's brunt,
> Hotly ye fell with all your wounds in front.
> That was your fame."

Not a line in the records of time for him. But there are other records—those of eternity. He has lost nothing of the thrill of life. He is being borne on that tide of self-surrender and heroism which has flowed through the ages, and bears those who embark on it to the very feet of God. He would not himself have it otherwise. "It is better far to go out with honour than survive with shame," wrote a comrade from the trenches, now united with him in death. There is a place for sorrow in our land, but its place is by the hearth-stones of those whose sons choose to survive with shame. He has taken his place among those who, unseen, are leading on the embattled hosts of his race to victory. He has discovered the treasures in store for the brave and the true. When, amid the flutterings of flags and the shouting of the people rejoicing in their deliverance, the great army will return home at last—he, too, will come.

At Kobé, when the bugles were welcoming the victorious Japanese home in 1895, Lafcadio Hearn spoke to an old man of those who would never return. "Probably the Western people believe," answered the old man, "that the dead never return. There are no Japanese dead who do not return. There are none who do not know the way." It is a poor, emasculated religion that does not believe that. When at the last the bugles call in the quiet evening ... they will come back. They will come crowned with glory and honour and immortality—with that victory which overcometh the world. Let the blinds be rolled up, and the windows be all flung open to the light.

# VI
# The Cities of the Plain

It was the old clerk, of whose services and devotion to our parish I have previously written, who gave the Biblical name to the little village that lies near the boundary of the great city that is steadily creeping towards us, and ever threatening to engulf us. Its own name is singularly pleasant to the ear and redolent of the sound of running waters, but it is unnecessary to burden the memory with it. Though it is now many years ago, I remember, as it were yesterday, the first time I heard the word on the old clerk's lips. I was sitting warming myself by the fire in the ticket-collector's office. The ticket-collector was ostensibly waiting to provide tickets, but as everybody in our parish has a season ticket, that part of his duty is almost a sinecure.

Thus it happens that the ticket-collector has leisure, just before the trains pass through, to give his friends the fruits of his researches in the realms of philosophy. That particular day he was speaking of the changes he had seen. "I was brought up," said he, closing his argument, "on the Shorter Catechism and porridge. I dinna haud any longer by the Catechism, but I havena lost my faith in porridge."

It was then that the clink of coppers was heard on the sill of the ticket window. In the aperture was framed the face of the clerk, with the trimmed grey beard and the small twinkling eyes. He held three pennies deftly in his thumbless hand. "Return, Sodom," said he. The ticket-collector pushed back his cap, stretched out his right hand as if he were beginning to speak, then thought better of it. Out of his case, without a word, he produced a return ticket for Sodom, clinked it in his machine, and passed it through the window. The old clerk received it with a grim chuckle.

Away below the bridge there came a rumble. "Train," said the ticket-collector, closing the aperture with a snap, and making for the door. And I have never forgotten the hoarse voice of the old clerk with an acid edge to it as he clinked his three coppers, saying "Return, Sodom."

It is an amazing thing how within the circuit of the same parish, removed by one mile from one another, there can live together two eras so remote from each other in the order of human development, as the world of the red-roofed houses on the slopes of the hills, and the village at their base where the gorge, worn by the little river through the travail of immemorial centuries, debouches on the great central plain that runs across Scotland.

Every morning the dwellers on the slopes are borne by the railway on a great span of arches over the little village, and they look down on the roofs of its houses. On the slopes there lies the world in which the fringes of life are embroidered—a world where men and women talk of books, pictures and plays. It is a world of hyphenated names. But in all the village there is not so much as one hyphenated name. It is a refuse-heap of humanity. Many diverse races are crowded in it. The city fathers clean out slums without providing first for the slum-dwellers, and, swept before the broom of so-called social reformers, homeless men and women have drifted to the village, and there reconstituted their slum.

From the glens of the north broken Highlanders, driven out to make room for sheep, have drifted hither to work in the quarries, and the speech of their children's children still bears the trace of their ancient language pure and clean; over the sea Irishmen have come to reap the harvest fields of the Lothians, and they have been deposited by the tide in the village. Stray Poles have come hither and straggling Czechs; a man from Connemara neighbours a shaggy giant from Lewis; and a dour stone-cutter from Aberdeen is door by door with an Italian who sells what looks like a deadly mixture from a hand-cart.

Here you can see humanity in its primitive state, before it began to adorn the fringes of life, and make for itself sanctuaries of privacy. Between the slopes and the base of the hill there yawns an invisible chasm. Centuries separate them. Thus it comes that the slope-dweller passes on the top of the arches, scanning his newspaper, without so much as seeing the huddle of houses which constitute the village.

It is only a week ago that, like the old clerk, I took out a return ticket for the "Cities of the Plain." (For the old clerk had a two-fold formula. When he was going to one village he said, "Return, Sodom," but when he meant to go to the quarries beside the village he said, "Return, Cities of the Plain.") It was to visit an old soldier that I thus descended into the plains. He lives in a rookery in which many families are crowded one on the top of the other—a rabbit-warren infested by many and strange odours. He used to come up the slopes and do odd jobs, tidying up gardens, and he loved to talk of

"unhappy far-off things
And battles long ago,"

in a language which I also could speak. So I got to know him. And as I sat by his bed I heard a moan from the adjoining room. It began in a low cry, and then rose into a wail that seemed charged with all the woes of humanity. The old man sat up in bed trembling. The cry of woe now changed into a chorus; other voices swelled it. It was the act of a moment to open the door, and in the dim landing find the door of this other room.

I opened it, and there I saw three children huddled before a grate which contained nothing but ashes. On an iron bed, stretched on straw, lay a woman sunk in sleep.... A foetid air was laden with the fumes of alcohol.... There was no food.... A broken chair, a stool or two, and a box that did duty for a table.... The old soldier told me what to do, and I did it. A kindly woman brought coal and food, and the wailing was silenced. The old man explained it all. The woman sunk in the stupor is the wife of a soldier now in the trenches. She did not belong to our parish; but only came a week or two before, swept before the broom of the "social reformers" from the city. The mothers of the Parish, the old soldier declared, were heroines. One such, when her son asked her consent to enlist, said, "Eh, laddie, I dinna want ye to gang; I dinna want ... but if I were ye I wud gang mysel'." Our own wives and mothers were splendid—but those who came from the city, flotsam and jetsam borne on the tide, staying for a little and then carried away again, of whom there were three or four in the village—these were different. They meet each other eager for news. They are depressed, and feel the need for cheering. One suggests a stimulant ... and the result is this.

He is no Puritan—the old soldier lying on his bed, his campaigning done—and he spoke out of an understanding heart. It was only poor human nature, overtaken by thick darkness and misery, trying to open a window towards the realm of sunshine.

And I came out into the roadway and turned towards the station. I did not see them before, but I saw them now. A few yards separating them, I pass two shops licensed to sell the means for opening windows towards this realm of happiness; and two houses with gaudy lights called the villagers to enter the region where all cares and worries are forgotten. In the street pale-faced, ill-clad children played at being soldiers, marching with heads erect. The gorge was already dark with the evening shadows, but the lamps in the village were lit.

When the village was passed I stood and looked back. In the west the setting sun had thrown over the heavens a glow. A well of liquid fire glowed over Torfionn, and its rays spread fan-like, so that they spanned the horizon, and, touching the rounded mass of Corstarfin, went forth over the firth. Against this background stood silhouetted the great arches that carry the railway across the hollow, and behind these the arches that bear the canal. The piers stood as a gigantic forest. These mighty arches might have been the work of the Romans. A soft, luminous haze fell on the village. Window after window was lit up. The door of a cottage near me was opened, and a flood of light streamed out. A woman stood in the door, and looking up the road shouted "Jim," and a little boy, leaving his fellow-soldiers, rushed to her, and she clasped him in her arms and closed the door.... In that moment the little village seemed to me as if it were an outpost of Paradise. Nature threw as a benediction the mantle of its loveliness over it. What nature meant to be a sanctuary of beauty, man had changed into Sodom.

The ticket-collector stood at his post and scanned the passengers as they went through. He knew them all, and had only a stray ticket to collect. I was last, and duly gave up my "return" from the "Cities of the Plain." But he did not let me through the gate. "I want to show you something," said the ticket-collector, and he led me into his office and produced a pamphlet.

"I got it from the man who goes to Keswick," said the ticket-collector; "you know him." I knew him, the best of men.

"Nae doubt," went on the ticket-collector; "nae doubt. He was always giving me tracts. Tracts—faugh!—poor stuff, nae style, nae logic, and nae philosophee in them. But I aye took them and thanked him—for he is a nice man, though a perfect babe in matters of understanding. And I found them useful for spills. The other day he handed me this..." and he waved a blue paper-covered booklet.

"Mahn," he exclaimed, pushing his peaked cap back from his grey head, and sweeping his brass buttons down with his hand; "mahn, this has fair hit me between the eyes." Then he opened the pamphlet and began to read passages that he had heavily scored with blue pencil. The Czar has abolished the sale of vodka for ever! What is the result?

"The old women in the villages," read the ticket-collector, "can hardly believe their own eyes, so changed are their menfolk.... Everywhere peace, kindness and industry. War is said to be hell; but this is like a foretaste of heaven."

"Listen to this," cried the collector, his arm outstretched. "A newspaper correspondent writes, since the sale of vodka stopped the old night population (in the doss-houses) seems to have vanished." Every passage he read bore the same testimony.

"And what are we doing?" he exclaimed. "We have stopped nothing; we surround our soldiers with the old temptations, and we leave their defenceless wives exposed to the same temptations; I know all about it.

Mahn, it was Ruskin that said, 'There is no wealth but life,' and we leave all our wealth of life at the mercy of every evil. It's a fair scandal. Do you ken the conclusion I've come to! It is that the best form of government is a benevolent despotism. Oor men are afraid of this and that—losing votes— but an autocrat with a stroke of a pen can sweep away the power of hell. If they would only make King George an autocrat for a few years.... That would be grand!"

He insisted on lending me the blue-covered pamphlet, and it being his hour off he walked with me across the bridge. The valley was now dark. The snuff-manufacturer's house down below was wrapped in gloom. Lights twinkled on the slopes. Below a lamp-post at the far end of the bridge two men stood. When he saw them the ticket-collector stood fast.

"Mahn," said he, "I've come to a great resolution. I'm too old to fight; and they canna get at me in ony way. No Income-tax for me; and threepence on the tea is naething, for I never take it; I want to feel that I am worth men dying for me; and I am going to be tee-total till the end of the war. I'll give the money to help the soldiers' weans. It's the weans that pull at my heart-strings."

And he turned on his heel and walked rapidly back across the bridge.

Under the lamp-post stood the roadman and the beadle, looking after him. I spoke to them, for since the war began we all speak to each other in our parish.

"Has he forgotten ony thin'?" asked the roadman, waving a hand towards the retreating form of the ticket-collector.

"I don't think so," I answered, "he just said that he was going to be tee-total till the end of the war."

"Tee-total!" echoed the roadman mournfully; "there gangs anither lost soul!"

My two friends went sadly down the steep brae, and I turned up the long flight of stone steps that leads to the road above. On the top of the first flight I turned and looked after them. When they came opposite the door of the village inn, they slowed down ... and then went resolutely past, down into the hollow. The two of them have probably resolved to join the company of the "lost souls."

I have read the ticket-collector's pamphlet, and I feel a little dazed. It is such an odd world, and the strange thing is that I never realised its queerness before. A Grand Duke is murdered in a place of which I never heard before, and whose name I cannot even now trust myself to write down correctly,

and here, a thousand miles away, the result is that I am brought face to face
for the first time with the problem that lay twice a day under my feet—the
problem of the Cities of the Plain. A flood of light seems to have fallen on
things which were aforetime hazy. Events stand out luridly and arrestingly.
Here is one. I was in a far Hebridean isle when war broke out. All of a
sudden there sounded the drum,

> "Saying Come,
> Freemen, come,
> Ere your heritage be wasted! said the
> quick alarming drum."

And the manhood of the island sprang to their feet. Mothers gave their
sons, sending them away with sobs and tears, but in the name of God.

On a drizzling morning the little steamer lay at the pier, crowded with
men and horses, going out to fight and die. The hawsers were loosed. The
steamer churned and backed and crept away. A girl stood near me crying
softly. A youth with clean-cut features, and the yearning no tongue can utter
shining in his eyes, leant over the taffrail and called to her, "Not crying,
Jessie?" And she wiped her cheek with the moist handkerchief, and turned
a smiling face to him and said, "No, I am not crying." And the paddles
churned faster, and they passed into the drizzle and the haze. Weeks later
I read how one man of that regiment—the regiment of my own county—
killed another ... and a few days later I read that he had done so in a drunken
brawl. He was not from the island, that man, and I know not who he is.
His mother doubtless sent him forth to fight as a hero for his King, and he
became a murderer under the fostering of the State.

Out of the clean countryside they were taken, these men, and the State
that summoned them, and whose call they answered, surrounded them with
temptations. Away from the influence of mother and sister and sweetheart,
wearied and worn with the hard toil of preparation, the State opened the
canteen and said, "Take your ease thus," and they did so. The Secretary
of War made appeals to them. "Be sober," said he, "avoid alcohol, that the
State, through your self-denial, may live." But the State said, "See, I have
made ample provision for you, so that you may disregard the noble advice
my servant gives you." They came in their thousands across the Atlantic
from the far North-West at the call of their mother—clean and sober—and
their mother opened the canteen for their benefit on the plain. Such a world
as that dwelt in the imagination of Dean Swift—I never imagined that it
could exist here and now. And in that world of the cities of the plain, what
reward are we preparing for the men who are baring their breasts to the
arrows, standing between us and death? When they come back, war-worn,

to what will they return? To homes in which the fires are extinguished, the candles burnt down to the socket; the cupboards bare, the children famished and neglected? Is that to be the guerdon of their sacrifice; is it for that that they have gone down into hell? Surely it cannot be for that! A wave has passed over us, raising us to the realisation of the higher values of things. Words live for us now which were dead yesterday. A beam of light has fallen into the chamber of imagery, and the word *Temperance* has risen from the couch on which it lay dying, and it claims us for its own. Through it we can make the world know that we are worth fighting for—worth that the young, the strong, and the brave should take everything they hold dear— their ideals, their love, their little children unborn—and throw them into the trench, and there give themselves and their dreams to death for us. We must see to it that we are worthy the sacrifice.

It seemed to me hitherto that I was a citizen of the country endowed with the greatest freedom on earth. But the ticket-collector has proved to me that that was a dream. Here in our parish I have no power to control this thing that matters so vitally in the Cities of the Plain. We have a Parish Council and a County Council, and I don't know how many other dignified and honourable authorities, whom we elect. But we elect nobody to control this. A body of unelected Justices, of whom we know nothing, settle for us that down yonder in the Cities of the Plain there shall be half a dozen State-regulated places for the manufacturing of paupers and criminals. (The laws change with such kaleidoscopic swiftness in those days that I may be wrong.) And here am I, newly awakened by the ticket-collector to that enormity, and I am not free to do anything. It is surely a mad world. We needed to be awakened; and we have been awakened with the shriek of shells and the crying of the perishing! And the result of the awakening will be regeneration for the Cities of the Plain.

The ticket-collector has deprived me for the time being of my peace of mind. My conversion is so recent that I am afraid of falling into the fanaticism of the newly converted. I followed the General the other day into the railway carriage, and as we were passing over Sodom, lying there under our feet, I spoke to him about it. He looked at me with cold eyes.

"Do you want to sacrifice the freedom of the individual?" he asked in his curt military tones; "do you think that you can make saints of people by Act of Parliament? They would be mere plaster-saints."

I was reduced to silence. My new-born zeal seemed to ooze out at every pore. There was a touch of amused scorn in the General's eye as he glanced at me. The General is a man of experience, and he is quite right. Acts of

Parliament will never make saints of the people. But the State can see to it that the people are not surrounded by temptations through the operations of Acts of Parliament; that, if the State is impotent to make saints, it shall not, on the other hand, set itself deliberately to make devils. That, it seems to me, is what the State is now doing in the Cities of the Plain.

In ten thousand schools the State sanctions that its children be taught to pray—"Lead us not into temptation," and that same State encircles the path of its children by legalised temptations at every corner. It is the maddest of worlds. I may be wrong and the General wholly right. But as the ticket-collector said the last time I saw him—"I would like to see the man who could convince me that I am wrong." And I don't know whether to be grateful to the ticket-collector or not. He has deprived me of some of my sleep; he has made my head ache with thinking of problems which I am not fit to cope with; and, most unlooked for of all, he has made a tee-totaler of me till the end of the war. There is a plaintive note in the ticket-collector's voice, which strikes a chord in my heart, when he invariably adds: "I hope the war won't last long." For, if it does, there will be the danger of the ticket-collector and myself becoming teetotalers for altogether. And it is such an ugly word—tee-totaler! If only the ticket-collector would coin a new and beautiful word to connote his new and beneficent state of mind! It is a pity that great causes should be burdened by the weight of ugly words.